CONTENTS

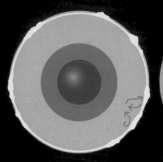
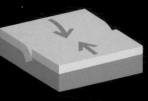
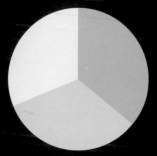

700033735771

WELCOME TO THE WORLD OF INFOGRAPHICS

Using icons, graphics and pictograms, infographics visualise data and information in a whole new way!

COMPARE THE TALLEST MOUNTAINS FROM EACH CONTINENT

SEE THE ENTIRE VOLUME OF WATER ON THE EARTH POURED INTO ONE GLASS

SEE HOW MANY TIMES THE 20 LONGEST RIVERS COULD WRAP AROUND THE EARTH

STACK UP EIFFEL TOWERS TO SEE HOW HIGH THE TALLEST WATERFALL IS

COMPARE THE WORLD'S LONGEST RIVERS

INSIDE THE EARTH

Slicing the entire Earth in half would show that its inside is divided into different layers. These layers push down on each other, creating high pressures and temperatures inside the planet.

CRUST

INNER AND OUTER CORE

MANTLE

0.4%

The crust makes up just 0.4 per cent of the Earth's mass, the core makes up about 30 per cent, while the mantle makes up nearly 70 per cent.

MANTLE 100 KM TO 2,900 KM

OUTER CORE 2,900 KM TO 5,100 KM

6,378 km

The distance from surface to the centre of the Earth (6,378 km) is the same as flying from London to Chicago.

The temperature inside the Earth increases with **depth**. This is called the **geothermal gradient**.

The pressures and temperatures inside the Earth are high enough to melt rock.

CRUST UP TO A DEPTH OF 100 KM

INNER CORE 5,100 KM TO 6,378 KM

MOLTEN ROCK IS CONSTANTLY ON THE MOVE

4,900–6,100°C

INNER CORE 4,900-6,100°C

OUTER CORE 4,500-5,000°C

SURFACE **AVERAGE 15°C**

The inner core is **as hot as** the surface of the **Sun**.

5

ON THE MOVE

The Earth's crust is broken up into tectonic plates. As the molten rock of the mantle swirls about under the crust, it pushes and pulls these plates around.

TRANSFORM BOUNDARY

where two plates rub against each other

DIVERGENT BOUNDARY

where two plates pull apart from each other

ARCTIC RIDGE

NORTH AMERICAN PLATE

JUAN DE FUCA PLATE

CARIBBEAN PLATE

AFRICAN PLATE

PACIFIC PLATE

COCOS PLATE

EAST PACIFIC RISE

NAZCA PLATE

SOUTH AMERICAN PLATE

SCOTIA PLATE

ANTARCTIC PLATE

Plate boundaries

The place where two plates meet is called a boundary. Plates rub together, pull apart or slam into each other. This movement of the crust between two plates can cause volcanic activity and earthquakes.

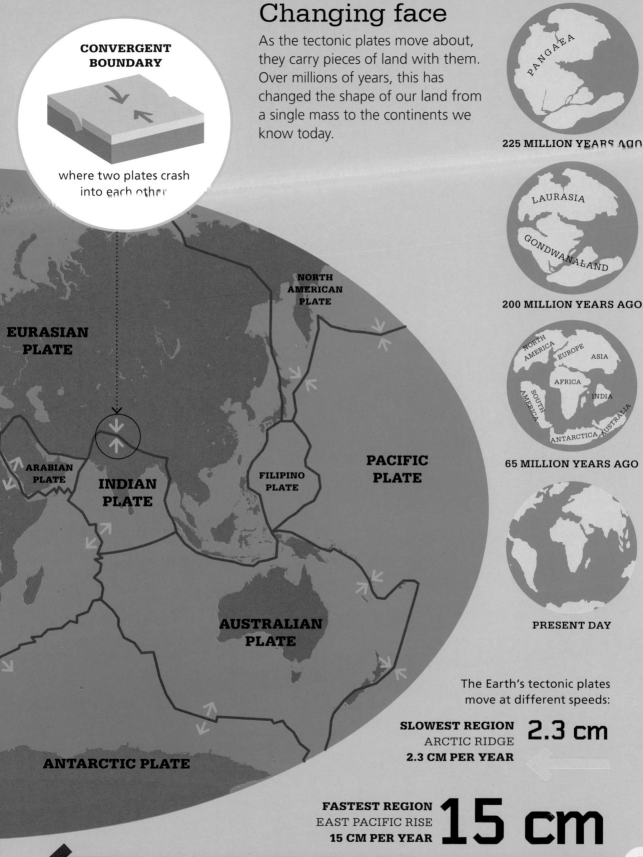

Changing face

As the tectonic plates move about, they carry pieces of land with them. Over millions of years, this has changed the shape of our land from a single mass to the continents we know today.

CONVERGENT BOUNDARY

where two plates crash into each other

PANGAEA

225 MILLION YEARS AGO

LAURASIA

GONDWANALAND

200 MILLION YEARS AGO

NORTH AMERICA
EUROPE
ASIA
AFRICA
SOUTH AMERICA
INDIA
ANTARCTICA
AUSTRALIA

65 MILLION YEARS AGO

PRESENT DAY

EURASIAN PLATE

NORTH AMERICAN PLATE

ARABIAN PLATE

INDIAN PLATE

FILIPINO PLATE

PACIFIC PLATE

AUSTRALIAN PLATE

ANTARCTIC PLATE

The Earth's tectonic plates move at different speeds:

SLOWEST REGION 2.3 cm
ARCTIC RIDGE
2.3 CM PER YEAR

FASTEST REGION 15 cm
EAST PACIFIC RISE
15 CM PER YEAR

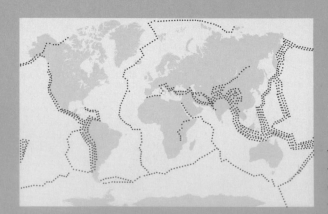

RESTLESS EARTH

The Earth's moving tectonic plates sometimes catch against each other and get stuck, before releasing suddenly. This sudden release causes earthquakes.

Strong or weak?

The strength of an earthquake is known as its magnitude. This is measured by the Richter scale – the higher the number, the stronger the earthquake. The scale has no upper limit, but no earthquake with a magnitude of 10 or higher has ever been recorded.

830,000

Death toll in the deadliest earthquake ever recorded. It occurred in the Shaanxi province of China in 1556.

7.8
1906 SAN FRANCISCO (USA)

8.0
1985 MEXICO CITY (MEXICO)

8.1
1650 CUZCO (PERU)

9.5
1960 VALDIVIA AND PUERTO MONTT (CHILE)

This map (left) highlights where major earthquakes occur. Most earthquakes occur at or near plate boundaries.

8.5

THE MOST POWERFUL NUCLEAR EXPLOSION, THE TSAR BOMBA, WAS DETONATED IN 1961. IT RELEASED THE SAME AMOUNT OF ENERGY AS AN EARTHQUAKE MEASURING 8.5 ON THE RICHTER SCALE.

MOST

Many countries can claim to have the most earthquakes, including Japan, Indonesia, Fiji, Tonga, China and Iran.

7.7
1780 TABRIZ (IRAN)

9.0
2011 HONSHU (JAPAN)

9.1
2004 ACEH PROVINCE (INDONESIA)

Of **500,000** earthquakes that are detected each year (several million actually occur each year), **100,000** can be felt and **100** cause any damage.

FEWEST

Small earthquakes can occur anywhere, but Antarctica is the continent with the fewest earthquakes.

MAGNITUDE	NUMBER
2–2.9	1,300,000
3–3.9	130,000
4–4.9	13,000
5–5.9	1,319
6–6.9	134
7–7.9	15
8.0+	1

NUMBER AND MAGNITUDE OF EARTHQUAKES PER YEAR

Every day, about

50

tonnes of rock is added to our planet from outer space – more than the weight of ten elephants! This falls to Earth as meteorites.

800–1,300°C

The temperature of magma when it comes to the surface, or erupts, from volcanoes.

LAVA COOLS TO FORM IGNEOUS ROCK

IGNEOUS ROCK

ROCKS SLOWLY PUSHED TO SURFACE

MAGMA COOLS

MAGMA

ROCKS BURIED, SQUEEZED AND HEATED

ROCKS MELT

METAMORPHIC ROCK

THE ROCK CYCLE

As the Earth's tectonic plates move about, rock is pushed down into the Earth, where it melts. Other rock is pushed up to the surface, where it is worn away or eroded by wind, ice and water. These changes in rocks are part of the rock cycle.

RAIN AND WIND ERODE ROCKS

ROCK PARTICLES TRANSPORTED BY RIVERS

ROCK PARTICLES FALL TO SEA FLOOR

LAYERS OF ROCK SQUEEZED TOGETHER

SEDIMENTARY ROCK

Rock types

There are three types of rock. Igneous rocks are formed from molten rock. Sedimentary rock is formed when tiny pieces of rock settle at the bottom of the sea where they are compressed. Metamorphic rock is formed when rocks are changed through heat and pressure.

80%

About 80 per cent of the rocks at the Earth's surface are sedimentary.

VIOLENT VOLCANOES

Volcanoes form when molten rock travels up from the Earth's mantle and erupts onto the surface. These eruptions can be quick and explosive or long and relatively peaceful.

TYPES OF VOLCANO

After lava erupts out of a volcano, it cools to form solid rock, creating the cone of the volcano. The shape of the cone depends on the type of lava. For example, runny lava creates a low, wide shield volcano.

SHIELD VOLCANO

COMPOUND/COMPLEX VOLCANO
WITH AN OLD CONE

STRATOVOLCANO

CALDERA VOLCANO

YELLOWSTONE
HUCKLEBERRY RIDGE
(2.1 MYA)
2,450 KM³
ENOUGH TO FILL
GREAT BEAR LAKE, CANADA

BIGGEST ERUPTIONS

This infographic shows the amount of magma produced by some of the biggest eruptions, along with their dates (MYA is 'millions of years ago'). The eruption at Toba was the largest ever.

ASH CLOUD

In 1991, the eruption of Mount Pinatubo sent an enormous cloud of ash to heights of 34 kilometres. The cloud covered an area of 125,000 sq km – that is about half the size of the UK.

THE EXPLOSION OF KRAKATOA IN 1883 HAD A FORCE EQUIVALENT TO

10,000

ATOMIC BOMBS

FORMING A CORAL ATOLL

1. Volcanic cone forms above sea level.

2. When volcano stops erupting, a ring of coral, called an atoll, forms around the cone.

3. Coral continues to grow, while the volcano cone is eroded.

4. Volcano cone eroded below sea level, leaving atoll above water.

YELLOWSTONE MESA FALLS (1.3 MYA)
280 KM³

LONG VALLEY CALDERA (760,000 YA)
600 KM³

YELLOWSTONE LAVA CREEK (640,000 YA)
1,000 KM³

TOBA

(74,000 YA)

2,800 KM³

ENOUGH TO FILL LAKE VICTORIA, AFRICA

TOWERING PEAKS

Where tectonic plates crash into each other, they can push the ground up to form mountains. Mountains are often grouped together in long chains near plate boundaries.

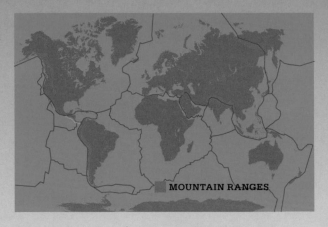

MOUNTAIN RANGES

← The tallest mountain in the world is part of the Himalayas mountain range.

This is the tallest peak in the Andes, which run the length of South America.

EVEREST
ASIA
8,848 m

ACONCAGUA
SOUTH AMERICA
6,962 m

ELBRUS
EUROPE
5,642 m

The tallest peak in Europe is a volcano that is part of the Caucasus range, which lies in Russia near the border with Georgia.

Changes

Conditions and climate change as you climb up a mountain, affecting the kinds of plants and animals that can live at different heights. Places that are higher up a mountain will be colder and may well be wetter that those lower down. Anything living here will have to adapt to these conditions.

ALPINE ZONE

SNOW LINE

TREE LINE

SUBALPINE ZONE
UP TO 3,970 m

TEMPERATE ZONE
UP TO 2,440 m

SUBTROPICAL ZONE
UP TO 1,830 m

16,000 km

The world's longest mountain range is the Mid-Atlantic Ridge. It runs along the entire length of the Atlantic Ocean and is completely submerged.

The tallest peak in North America was formed by a collision between the Pacific and North American plates.

Kilimanjaro is the highest peak in Africa and is not part of a mountain chain.

MT McKINLEY (DENALI)
NORTH AMERICA
6,194 m

KILIMANJARO
AFRICA
5,895 m

VINSON MASSIF
ANTARCTICA
4,897 m

Part of the Ellsworth Mountains, this peak is just 1,200 km from the South Pole.

CARSTENSZ PYRAMID
OCEANIA
4,884 m

Located on New Guinea, this mountain was formed by a collision between the Australian and Pacific plates.

HABITATS

From teeming coral reefs to densely packed forests, the world is covered in a wide range of different habitats. The type of habitat is decided by what the climatic conditions are in a region.

POLAR AND
TUNDRA

TEMPERATE
FOREST

SAVANNAH

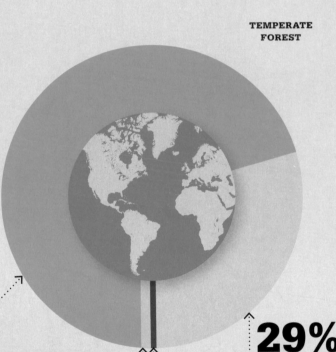

TROPICAL
FOREST

MOUNTAIN
VEGETATION

29%
OF EARTH
IS LAND

71%
OF EARTH
IS AQUATIC
OF WHICH...

1% IS COVERED BY
CORAL REEFS

2.5% IS FRESHWATER

29%
OF EARTH IS LAND
OF WHICH...

31% DESERT
INCLUDING THE POLES

33% GRASSLAND
INCLUDING TEMPERATE GRASSLAND AND SAVANNAH

36% FOREST
INCLUDING TROPICAL AND CONIFEROUS FOREST (TAIGA)

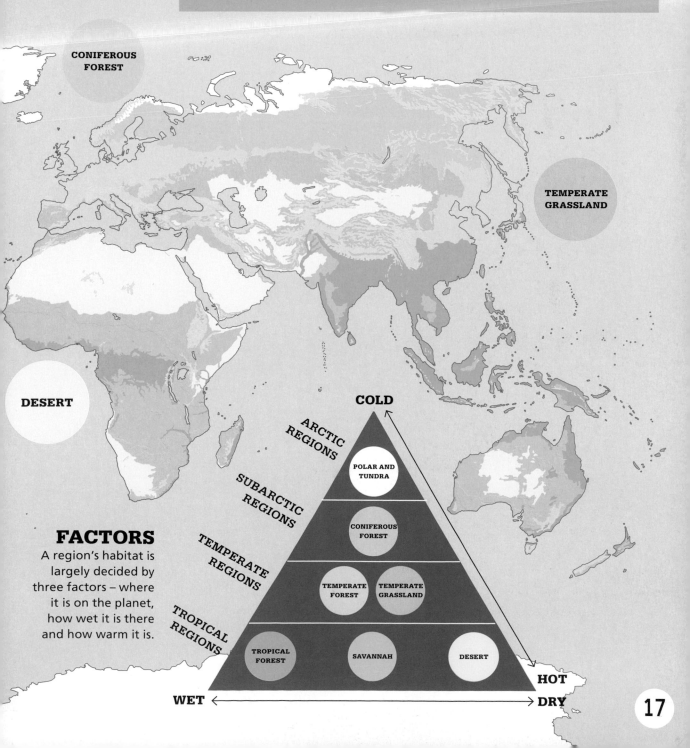

CONIFEROUS FOREST

TEMPERATE GRASSLAND

DESERT

FACTORS
A region's habitat is largely decided by three factors – where it is on the planet, how wet it is there and how warm it is.

COLD

ARCTIC REGIONS

POLAR AND TUNDRA

SUBARCTIC REGIONS

CONIFEROUS FOREST

TEMPERATE REGIONS

TEMPERATE FOREST

TEMPERATE GRASSLAND

TROPICAL REGIONS

TROPICAL FOREST

SAVANNAH

DESERT

HOT

WET ← → DRY

THE AIR WE BREATHE

Surrounding our planet is a thin layer of gases called the atmosphere. It contains the air that is vital for us to live and it produces all of our weather.

THERMOSPHERE
85–640 KM

MESOSPHERE
50–85 KM

SPACESHIPONE
FIRST MANNED PRIVATE
SPACEFLIGHT 112 KM

STRATO-LAB V
HIGHEST MANNED BALLOON 34 KM ·····>

STRATOSPHERE
18–50 KM

MODERN PASSENGER JET
CRUISING ALTITUDE 10 KM

CIRRUS

CIRROSTRATUS

ALTOCUMULUS

NIMBOSTRATUS

CUMULONIMBUS

STRATUS   CUMULUS

TROPOSPHERE
WITH CLOUDS
UP TO 18 KM

WIND SPEED

As air is heated by the Sun, it starts to move around, creating wind. Wind speed is measured using the Beaufort scale. A measure of one is almost still, while 12 will blow down buildings.

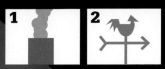

HUBBLE SPACE TELESCOPE
559 KM

EXOSPHERE
ABOVE 640 KM

ISS
278–460 KM

408 km/h

The fastest wind speed ever recorded. It was measured at an automatic weather station on Barrow Island, Australia, during tropical cyclone Olivia on 10 April 1996.

78.08%
NITROGEN

20.95%
OXYGEN

0–4%
WATER VAPOUR

0.93%
ARGON

0.038%
CARBON DIOXIDE

What's in air?

Most of the air we breathe in is made up of the gas nitrogen. About one-fifth of air is made up of oxygen, which is the gas we need to stay alive. There are also tiny amounts of other gases, including argon and carbon dioxide.

WATER CYCLE

Water is vital for life. It also plays an important part in the weather and in shaping the land. Water moves around our planet in a system called the water cycle.

1,000,000,000,000,000

EACH DAY, THE SUN CAUSES ONE TRILLION TONNES OF WATER TO EVAPORATE.

CONDENSATION

80%
OF THE EARTH'S WATER IS SURFACE WATER.

20% IS EITHER GROUNDWATER OR ATMOSPHERIC WATER VAPOUR

TRANSPIRATION
FROM PLANTS

EVAPORATION
FROM OCEANS AND LAKES

505,000 KM³

The volume of water that falls as precipitation each year all around the Earth.

PRECIPITATION

SNOW MELT

434,000 KM³

The amount of water that evaporates from the Earth's oceans in a year.

Nearly **all** of the water found in the atmosphere lies within the **troposphere**, the part of the atmosphere below **18 km**.

SURFACE RUNOFF

GROUNDWATER

OCEANS AND LAKES

3%

The average amount of salt and minerals found in seawater.

WATER WORLD

Water covers 71 per cent of the Earth's surface, in seas, oceans and rivers. But water is also found in the air we breathe and frozen in the ice caps near the poles. Just how much water is there on our planet?

1.4 BILLION KM³

The total volume of all the water on our planet and in the atmosphere.

EARTH'S DIAMETER 12,756 KM

IF THE WORLD'S WATER WERE MADE INTO A BALL, IT WOULD MEASURE 1,390 KM ACROSS. ················>

ICEBERG B15 295 KM LONG

The world's largest iceberg, called B15, broke away from Antarctica in 2000. Parts of it still haven't melted.

JAMAICA 234 KM LONG

MASS OF ICEBERG B15 WAS THREE BILLION TONNES **3,000,000,000**

FRESHWATER 2.5%
OF THIS...

SALTWATER IN
OCEANS, SEAS,
GROUNDWATER
AND LAKES

97.5%

GLACIERS
68.7%

GROUNDWATER
30.1%

PERMANENTLY FROZEN IN THE
GROUND (PERMAFROST) **0.8%**

WATER IN THE AIR AND ON THE
EARTH'S SURFACE **0.4%**

RAINFALL RECORDS

Most in one minute: 31.2 mm; Unionville, Maryland, USA, 4 July 1956

Most in 60 minutes: 305 mm in 42 minutes; Holt, Missouri, USA, 22 June 1947

Most in 12 hours: 1,144 mm; Foc-Foc, Réunion, 8 January 1966, during tropical cyclone Denise

Most in 24 hours: 1,825 mm; Foc-Foc, Réunion, 7–8 January 1966

Most in 48 hours: 2,467 mm; Aurère, Réunion, 8–10 January 1958

Most in 72 hours: 3,929 mm; Commerson, Réunion, 24–26 February 2007

Most in 96 hours: 4,869 mm; Commerson, Réunion, 24–27 February 2007

Most in one year: 26,470 mm; Cherrapunji, India, 1860–1861

Highest average annual total: 11,872 mm; Mawsynram, India

SCUBA DIVING 330 M

FREE DIVING 273 M

ATMOSPHERIC DIVING SUIT 610 M

1,000 M

MILITARY SUBMARINE 1,300 M

SPERM WHALE
3,000 M

ANGLERFISH
3,000 M

COLOSSAL SQUID
2,200 M

WRECK OF TITANIC
3,780 M

4,000 M

THE OCEANS

Beneath the surface of the Earth's seas and oceans is a varied world of different regions that reach down to the darkest depths.

CUSK-EEL
8,370 M

8,000 M

Under pressure

The oceans are divided into different zones. The photic zone is part of the ocean where sunlight can reach. Beneath it is the dark aphotic zone. Pressures become greater as depths increase. Just 10 m below the waves, the pressure is already twice that at the surface.

THE SUBMERSIBLE *TRIESTE* HOLDS THE RECORD FOR THE DEEPEST DIVE EVER MADE – 10,911 M BELOW THE SURFACE.

TRIESTE

10,911 M

46.5%

The percentage of the world's oceans made up by the Pacific – almost as much as the Indian, Atlantic, Southern and Arctic Oceans put together.

6% · · · · · · · ·
SOUTHERN OCEAN

4.1%
ARCTIC OCEAN

20.5%
INDIAN OCEAN

22.9%
ATLANTIC OCEAN

46.5%
PACIFIC OCEAN

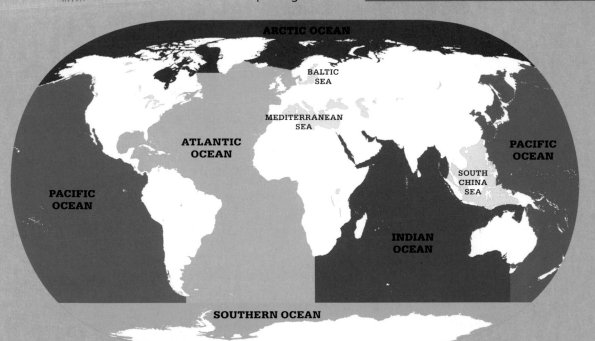

ARCTIC OCEAN

BALTIC SEA

MEDITERRANEAN SEA

ATLANTIC OCEAN

PACIFIC OCEAN

SOUTH CHINA SEA

PACIFIC OCEAN

INDIAN OCEAN

SOUTHERN OCEAN

If all the **salt** were taken out of the ocean it would cover all the land to a depth of

1.5 metres

The deepest part of the ocean is deeper than the highest peak on Earth.

MOUNT EVEREST
8,848 METRES HIGH

CHALLENGER DEEP
11,035 METRES BELOW SEA LEVEL

RAGING RIVERS

Some of the Earth's rivers are so big that they stretch for thousands of kilometres. They tumble over towering waterfalls and meander through the countryside, carrying enormous amounts of water across the land.

	source	countries crossed
NILE	LAKE VICTORIA	ETHIOPIA SUDAN SOUTH SUDAN EGYPT UGANDA TANZANIA RWANDA DEMOCRATIC REPUBLIC OF THE CONGO KENYA BURUNDI ERITREA
AMAZON-UCYALO-APURIMAC	ANDES MOUNTAINS	BRAZIL COLOMBIA ECUADOR PERU
YANGTZE	TANGGULA MOUNTAINS	CHINA
MISSISSIPPI-MISSOURI-RED ROCK	LAKE ITASCA	UNITED STATES
YENISEY-BAIKAL-SELENGA	MUNGARAGIYN-GOL	MONGOLIA RUSSIA
HUANG HE (YELLOW)	BAYAN HAR MOUNTAINS	CHINA
OB-IRTYSH	BELUKHA MOUNTAIN	RUSSIA
PARANÁ	RIO PARANAÍBA	ARGENTINA BRAZIL PARAGUAY
	source	countries crossed

River discharge

The amount of water that a river releases into a sea or lake is called its discharge. A river's discharge depends on the local climate and the size of its drainage basin, which is the area of land that the river empties of water.

The world's **20** largest rivers **discharge** enough water to fill a **football stadium** in **3** seconds.

RIVERS WITH THE GREATEST DISCHARGE

RIO NEGRO
28,400 m³/s

MADEIRA
31,200 m³/s

ORINOCO
33,000 m³/s

YANGTZE
35,000 m³/s

250,000

The number of rivers there are in the USA, with a combined total length of more than 5.6 million kilometres.

If you put the 20 longest rivers end to end they would wrap around the equator more than

twice

ends	length
MEDITERRANEAN SEA	6,650 km
ATLANTIC OCEAN	6,400 km
EAST CHINA SEA	6,300 km
GULF OF MEXICO	5,971 km
YENISEI GULF	5,540 km
BOHAI SEA	5,465 km
GULF OF OB	5,410 km
RIO DE LA PLATA	4,880 km
ends	length

CONGO
41,200 m³/s

GANGES
42,470 m³/s

AMAZON
175,000 m³/s

Angel Falls, Venezuela **979 m**

3 Eiffel Towers

HIGHEST WATERFALL IN THE WORLD

CHANGING EARTH

Conditions on our planet are not fixed. During the Earth's history there have been long periods of the planet heating up and then cooling down. Scientists have discovered that, at present, the Earth is getting warmer.

REFLECTED
Some of the Sun's radiation is reflected back out into space by the Earth's surface.

LOST HEAT
When the Earth absorbs the Sun's radiation, it then produces its own radiation as infrared heat. Some of this heat is lost into space.

Rising seas

Increasing temperatures around the world could melt the ice caps at the poles. As a result, sea levels would rise. The red areas on the graphic above are those that would be flooded by a rise in sea levels of 100 m.

AEROSOLS

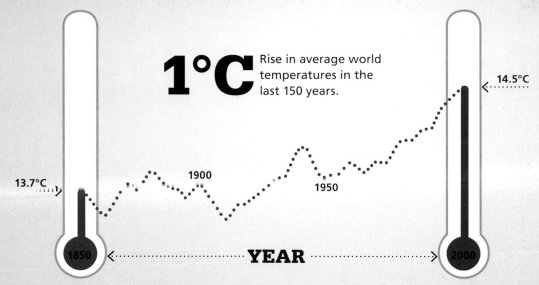

1°C Rise in average world temperatures in the last 150 years.

14.5°C

13.7°C

1900

1950

1850

YEAR

2000

Warming

Our planet is kept warm by a process called the greenhouse effect. Gases and other substances, such as aerosols, in the atmosphere trap the heat that is reflected or given off by the Earth.

SUN'S RAYS

Nearly three-quarters of the Sun's radiation that reaches the Earth makes it to the surface.

AEROSOLS

LOST IN SPACE

Some of the Sun's radiation is reflected straight back out into space.

GREENHOUSE

Gases and other substances in the atmosphere trap heat given off by the Earth, warming the atmosphere up even more and creating the greenhouse effect.

29

GLOSSARY

Continents
Large areas of land. The Earth has seven continents: Asia, Africa, North America, South America, Europe, Australia and Antarctica.

Core
The mass that lies at the centre of the Earth. It is divided up into the outer core, which is 2,200 km thick, and an inner core, which has a radius of about 1,300 km.

Crust
The outermost layer of the Earth. The Earth's crust is up to 100 km thick.

Igneous
A type of rock that forms from the cooling of magma or lava.

Drainage basin
An area of land that a river drains of water. Rain that falls within this area will flow over or under the ground, collecting together to form streams. These streams will then join together to form the larger river.

Lava
When magma reaches the Earth's surface during a volcanic eruption, it is called lava.

Greenhouse effect
The process by which the atmosphere traps heat given off by the Earth before it can escape into space. This trapped heat warms up the atmosphere.

Magma
Molten rock that is found beneath the Earth's surface.

Magnitude
How strong something is. For example, the magnitude of an earthquake is measured by the Richter scale – a higher reading on this scale indicates a stronger earthquake.

Mantle
The region inside the Earth that lies beneath the crust and above the core. It reaches down to a depth of 2,900 km below the surface and is made up of hot, molten rock.

Metamorphic
A type of rock that has been created under extreme heat and pressure.

Molten
A substance that has become liquid by getting very hot. For example, the metal iron becomes molten at 1,538°C.

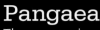

Pangaea
The name given to the enormous piece of land formed on Earth 270 million years ago.

Precipitation
Water that falls to the ground as rain or snow.

Radiation
A type of energy that is released in wave form, such as light, or as tiny subatomic particles.

Richter scale
The scale used to measure the strength of an earthquake – the higher the number the more powerful the tremor.

Sedimentary
A type of rock that is formed by small rock particles that have settled from water and been squashed together.

Subalpine zone
A region that lies just below the tree line on the side of a mountain.

Subarctic zone
The region that lies between the Arctic and the temperate regions.

Taiga
A type of coniferous forest that is found in a large band south of the Arctic, running through North America, northern Europe and Russia.

Tectonic plates
The large pieces of the Earth's surface that fit together to form the crust. These pieces are crashing into each other, pulling apart or rubbing against one another.

Transpiration
When plants give off water vapour.

Tributary
A small river that flows into a larger one.

Websites

MORE INFO:
www.metoffice.gov.uk
Website of the UK's Meteorological Office. It contains information on current weather conditions around the world, as well as global climate patterns.

www.noaa.gov
Home page of the National Oceanic and Atmospheric Administration, including an education section for teachers and students.

www.usgs.gov
The US Geological Survey studies the state of the world's habitats and environment as well as natural hazards, such as earthquakes.

MORE GRAPHICS:
www.visualinformation.info
A website that contains a whole host of infographic material on subjects as diverse as natural history, science, sport and computer games.

www.coolinfographics.com
A collection of infographics and data visualisations from other online resources, magazines and newspapers

www.dailyinfographic.com
A comprehensive collection of infographics on an enormous range of topics that is updated every single day!

INDEX

ACKNOWLEDGEMENTS

First published in 2012 by Wayland

Copyright © Wayland 2012

Wayland
338 Euston Road
London NW1 3BH

Wayland Australia
Level 17/207 Kent Street
Sydney NSW 2000

All rights reserved.
Senior editor: Julia Adams

Produced by Tall Tree Ltd
Editor: Jon Richards
Designer: Ed Simkins
Consultant: John Williams

British Library Cataloguing in Publication Data
Richards, Jon, 1970-
  The world in infographics.
  Planet Earth.
  1. Earth--Pictorial works--Juvenile literature.
  I. Title II. Planet Earth III. Simkins, Ed.
  550-dc23
  ISBN: 9780750269018
Printed in China

Wayland is a division of Hachette
Children's Books, an Hachette UK company.
www.hachette.co.uk

The website addresses (URLs) included in this
book were valid at the time of going to press.
However, because of the nature of the Internet,
it is possible that some addresses may have
changed, or sites may have changed or closed
down, since publication. While the author and
Publisher regret any inconvenience this may
cause the readers, no responsibility for any such
changes can be accepted by either the author
or the Publisher.

the world in infographics

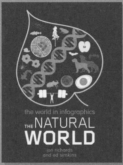

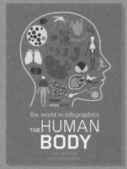

beautifully visualised information